# In Full Bloom

## A THINKING APPROACH TO TEACHING LITERATURE

# TINA McDOUGALL

**HAWKER BROWNLOW**
EDUCATION

To Michael and Jaimee: may their love of literature never cease.

**Cover & Book Designer:** Eva Ming Ling Kam
**Editor:** Margaret Maher

Published in Australia by
**HAWKER BROWNLOW**
E D U C A T I O N

© 2003 Hawker Brownlow Education
P.O. Box 580, Moorabbin,
Victoria 3189, Australia
Phone: (03) 9555 1344 Fax: (03) 9553 4538
Toll Free Ph: 1800 33 4603 Fax: 1800 15 0445
Website: http://www.hbe.com.au
Email: brown@hbe.com.au

All rights reserved
Printed in Australia

Code: #HB-9653

0703

National Library of Australia Cataloguing-in-Publication entry:

McDougall, Tina.
In full Bloom: a thinking approach to teaching literature.
ISBN 1 74025 569 0.

1. Bloom, Benjamin S. (Benjamin Samuel), 1913– . 2.
Literature – Study and teaching (Primary). I. Title.

372.64

# Contents

#HB-9653 © 2003 Hawker Brownlow Education

# Introduction

*I*n Full Bloom: A Thinking Approach to
Teaching Literature is designed to help
teachers create a community of
lifelong readers. It promotes insightful
analysis through creative problem-solving and
thought-provoking tasks based on Bloom's
Taxonomy. In providing a model and guide
for teachers to individualise the teaching of
reading in their classroom, *In Full Bloom* helps
teachers to develop and extend their students'
literacy skills and understandings about texts
through the use of 'real books'.

# Overview

*I*n Full Bloom: A Thinking Approach to Teaching Literature *is designed to help teachers create a community of lifelong readers. It promotes insightful analysis through creative problem-solving and thought-provoking tasks based on Bloom's Taxonomy. In providing a model and guide for teachers to individualise the teaching of reading in their classroom,* In Full Bloom *helps teachers to develop and extend their students' literacy skills and understandings about texts through the use of 'real books'.*

Teachers can help their students improve their level of literacy by providing them with opportunities to engage with language that is meaningful, interesting and enjoyable. It is important, therefore, that teachers organise a rich, literature-filled environment for all their students so that the process of reading is nurtured.

*In Full Bloom* is divided into four main parts.

**Part one** provides a brief introduction to Bloom and his learning domains. It gives teachers an explanation of each of the six levels of Bloom's cognitive domain, and provides keywords and phrases to use at each level when teaching and assessing each student's level of understanding. It also lists the tasks appropriate for each level.

**Part two** suggests a way of implementing a reading program during a one-hour reading session, using the following procedure.

*Engaging* gives an overview of the types of activities teachers could introduce to their students at the beginning of each session. These activities are intended to teach children how to respond to texts in a variety of meaningful ways.

*Responding* discusses the main part of the lesson. It explains the use of conferences and how the 'teaching' group fits within this model of teaching. It offers practical suggestions on how to teach the skills students will need to be able to read with meaning and clarity.

*Presenting* this section emphasises and explains the importance of giving the students time to present their work to their peers and to a wider audience.

**Part three** contains 60 independent reading tasks, ten for each level of Bloom's cognitive domain. The tasks require the students to think about aspects of story structure. Many of the tasks within the program incorporate information communication technologies. Students are encouraged to use a number of multimedia tools to publish their responses to the texts. The tasks also promote the use of online learning with opportunities for children to explore the Internet for relevant sites to assist them in their literature pursuits.

**Part four** suggests ways of assessing students' performance in literacy. It provides information on creating checklists, student reading journals, gathering work samples and using conferences and presentations to collect anecdotal evidence of students' performance and level of understanding. It also provides six checklists containing all the tasks for teachers to keep track of activities their students have completed and a list of questions teachers can use during a conference to determine their students' understanding of story structure.

 #HB-9653 © 2003 Hawker Brownlow Education

# Benjamin Bloom's Taxonomy

Benjamin Bloom was a lecturer and practical theorist in the field of education. He displayed a passion for the inquiry process and believed that human potential could be further developed through education. He was interested in exploring ways in which higher-order thinking could be promoted in educational settings.

Bloom believed that the environment also influenced a learner's potential and performance. If a child was supported and given ample opportunities to succeed in a positive environment then learning would take place as a matter of course. Attainment of goals would happen as a natural consequence rather than from some predetermined genetic ability. Bloom maintained that individual differences arose because of these varied environments and that teachers should assist students to achieve the outcomes of the curriculum by accommodating individual differences. It made no sense to Bloom to have all students working on the same task at the same time and then wait for some students to fail. Teaching tasks had to be designed in a way that would allow all children to achieve success.

Bloom's research into 'gifted children' provides further insights into how children learn. Studies of children whose parents provided interactive experiences, positive habits, values and attitudes showed that these children were likely to succeed at school. While Bloom acknowledged that some children demonstrated special abilities, he believed that the teacher's role was to provide optimum learning conditions for all students so that children from not-so-privileged backgrounds had the chance to succeed as well.

Further study into academic performance led Bloom to make certain observations. He found that at around seven years of age, a child's academic assessments could be analysed and predictions about the child's academic standing in early adolescence could be made. However, Bloom did not regard this as an impediment. He believed that with proper instruction and intervention teachers could significantly alter student performance. The implications of this study on teaching and learning are profound. Differentiating the curriculum to take into account varying abilities and learning needs is of paramount importance if we are to assist our students to achieve learning outcomes. What is also clear is that students need time to work through tasks that encourage higher-order thinking, not merely the regurgitation of facts.

Bloom is mostly known for his research and subsequent findings of several intellectual behaviours considered critical to the process of learning. These behaviours were divided into three interdependent learning domains and became known as Bloom's Taxonomy.

# The Learning Domains

The learning domains of Bloom's taxonomy cover cognitive learning, affective learning and psychomotor learning. A brief description of each is given below.

## *Cognitive Learning*

This level of learning is concerned with the six levels of critical thinking as identified by Bloom. In this domain learners observe and recall information; show ways of organising ideas and solving problems; collect, then analyse and synthesise data; and evaluate ideas, arguments and theories.

## *Affective Learning*

This level of learning is concerned with the attitudes, emotions and values of the learner. Indications of this type of learning include such behaviours as interest and motivation, the learner's ability to listen actively, levels of awareness and the way learners interact with other learners.

## *Psychomotor Learning*

This level of learning incorporates all physical skills. It includes such physical behaviours as coordination, manipulation, strength, flexibility, skill, speed, and fine and gross motor skills.

The purpose of this book is to explore the use of the cognitive domain in the teaching of reading. This is the domain which contains Bloom's six levels of critical thinking. These levels (knowledge, comprehension, application, analysis, synthesis and evaluation) are discussed in more detail on the following pages.

# The Cognitive Domain in Teaching

Bloom's cognitive domain, which contains six categories of the acquisition and use of knowledge, can be used as a model for teaching critical, creative and analytical thinking skills as well as a model for constructivist approaches to learning in the classroom. (See the examples on pages 15 and 16.)

Using the cognitive domain in the reading program will enable students to move beyond merely recalling and understanding a collection of facts to solving complex problems, recognising hidden meanings, drawing conclusions, comparing and discriminating, and assessing the value of theories and arguments.

Over time, student responses will become more sophisticated as they develop confidence and a willingness to take risks with this new approach. They will learn to think independently, and the teacher's role is to facilitate this process.

Because of the way it is structured, Bloom's cognitive domain is an ideal tool to use when planning and implementing a learning-oriented reading program. Students move through the various levels, building upon each experience as they acquire new information and knowledge. Key words and phrases introduced at each level are helpful when creating questions and activities for students. They can be used to formulate questions for a class discussion following the reading of a story or to assess a particular thinking process, for instance synthesis. Group tasks or individual student contracts centred on a topic or idea can be structured in a way that allows students to be monitored as they explore the process of knowledge construction.

This domain enables teachers to differentiate the reading program to take into account their students' varying abilities and learning needs. The teacher's challenge is then to set up an environment that promotes individual growth and cognitive development.

Students need to be encouraged to interact with other students in their class and be given the opportunity to discuss and debate their findings and new understandings so that analytical and creative thought can take place. Open discussions that respect the ideas put forth by students will encourage risk taking and develop students' problem-solving skills as they make new connections through the process of defending their views and opinions. When students are given the chance to express an alternative point of view as well as listening to the views of others, they will acquire a solid knowledge base to build upon.

Bloom's cognitive domain has a prominent role to play in the student-centred, learning-oriented classroom. In order for students to construct their own meaning and develop reflective thought processes, teachers must create an environment that will allow this to occur. By using Bloom's cognitive domain, teachers can be assured that their students will be given the necessary tools to become explicit in their thinking and make insightful judgements about their learning.

The following section gives some basic information about each of the levels of Bloom's cognitive domain, as well as some examples of key words, skills and tasks for each area.

# The Levels of the Cognitive Domain

## *Knowledge*

This level of thinking involves the recall of facts. It requires learners to remember factual information and tests their ability to recall and recognise.

| Key Words and Skills for this Level | Phrases to Assess Understanding at this Level | Tasks |
|---|---|---|
| List | Read the story of … Who were the main characters? | **Readers' Theatre** Read a story aloud. |
| Label | | |
| Name | Paint a picture of … that shows … | **Felt Board** Recreate a story with felt characters. |
| Describe | | |
| Define | Name some … | |
| Memorise | | **Postcard** Interpret a descriptive passage. |
| Recite | Make a facts chart that lists … | |
| State | Label the parts of … | **Slide Show** Create a slide show describing the plot, characters and setting. |
| Identify | | |
| Show | Locate the meaning of … | |
| Examine | Arrange these sentences. | **Story Map** List the events in the story. |
| Quote | Group these objects according to … | |
| Find | | **Storyteller** Read the story to a younger audience. |
| Recognise | Give a brief outline of … | |
| Select | Match these … with … | **Word Puzzles** Create your own crosswords or word searches. |
| Order | Underline all the … | |
| Arrange | | |
| Repeat | Draw a flow chart to show the … | **Bookmark** Make a bookmark, complete with title, author, illustrator and blurb. |
| Group | | |
| Match | Make a list of … | |
| Outline | Is … true or false? | **Story Poster** Illustrate an exciting part of the story. |
| Collect | | |
| Record | | |
| Underline | | **Character Mobiles** Describe character traits. |
| Review | | |

 #HB-9653 © 2003 Hawker Brownlow Education

# Comprehension

This level of thinking involves showing an understanding of the information that has been recalled. It requires learners to interpret and explain facts.

| Key Words and Skills for this Level | Phrases to Assess Understanding at this Level | Tasks |
|---|---|---|
| Restate | Compare and contrast … | **Who's Who** Compare and contrast two characters from the same story. |
| Locate | Retell the story in your own words. | **Talkfest** Write a brief conversation between two characters. |
| Discuss | | |
| Explain | Summarise this passage and then create a new title for it. | **Lift the Flap** Make a 'lift the flap' chart identifying important information about the plot, characters and setting. |
| Tell | What does this mean? | |
| Outline | Explain why … | |
| Identify | Give an example of … | **Keeping Track** Use a flowchart to illustrate a sequence of events. |
| Compare | | |
| Generalise | Substitute this phrase with one word. | **Game Time** Make up questions about the plot, character, setting etc. |
| Change | What is … trying to say? | |
| Match | Which sentence supports … ? | **Fave Rave** Illustrate favourite sentences from a story. |
| Illustrate | What seems to be the … | |
| Classify | Explain what is happening in this … | **Design a Set** Design a set for a play based on a scene from a story. |
| Show | | |
| Select | Can you predict what will happen? | **Comic Capers** Choose a story and rewrite it in cartoon format. |
| Represent | | |
| Group | Discuss the difference between … and … | **Character Traits** Write a list of words and phrases that aptly describe a character. |
| Summarise | | |
| Describe | Write a brief outline explaining … | |
| Predict | Match the … with … | **Acting Up!** Rewrite a story as a script. |

# *Application*

This level of thinking involves using previously learned information and skills to solve new problems. It requires learners to use information in new situations and in the correct context.

| Key Words and Skills for this Level | Phrases to Assess Understanding at this Level | Tasks |
|---|---|---|
| Interpret | What would the result be if … | **Holidays!** Turn the story setting into a holiday destination. |
| Apply | Can you predict what would happen if … | |
| Interview | | **Let's Celebrate** Organise a party for the main character. |
| Record | Can you think of an example when … | |
| Produce | | **On the Scene Reporter** Retell the story as a news report. |
| Show | Show how … | |
| Solve | Create a set of instructions that … | **Playing Games** Create a board game based on the story. |
| Demonstrate | | |
| Construct | Construct a model which shows … | **Puppet Show** Retell the story as a puppet show. |
| Create | Classify … according to … | |
| Use | Make a collection of … to demonstrate or prove … | **Windows into Worlds** Make a diorama of a scene from the story. |
| Complete | | |
| Examine | Use the information gathered to show how … could be modified. | |
| Modify | | **A Model Character** Create a 3-D model of a character. |
| Change | Make a list of questions that could be used when interviewing … | |
| Classify | | **Cover Up!** Make a dust jacket for the book. |
| Select | Imagine that you … Describe what … | |
| Model | | **Story Starters** Make a list of suitable story starters. |
| Prove | Examine … to find out … | |
| Dramatise | | **Word Collage** Construct a collage about the story. |

# *Analysis*

This level of thinking involves breaking down information into smaller parts. It requires learners to examine these parts and recognise hidden meanings and relationships.

| Key Words and Skills for this Level | Phrases to Assess Understanding at this Level | Tasks |
|---|---|---|
| Distinguish | What conclusions can you make after …? | **What Are they Really Like?** Compile an A to Z of words that describe a character. |
| Investigate | | |
| Survey | What is the purpose of …? | |
| Debate | Can you distinguish between … and …? | **Wanted!** Create a wanted poster. |
| Organise | What assumptions can be made about …? | **Under the Microscope** A 'plus, minus, interesting' table. |
| Question | | |
| Inquire | What is … point of view? | **Step Right Up!** Create an advertisement to promote the story. |
| Compare | Are there inconsistencies in the …? | |
| Group | | |
| Analyse | What is the main idea … | **Maybe … Maybe Not …** Distinguish between fact and fiction. |
| Contrast | What is the relationship between … and …? | **I Wonder What Would Happen If …** Write a different solution to a conflict. |
| Explain | | |
| Arrange | What conclusions can you make after reading …? | |
| Infer | How is … different to …? | **Dear Author** Write to the author. |
| Notice | Explain why … | |
| Break down | What was the problem with …? | **Back to the Past** Describe a setting. |
| Examine | | |
| Inquire | Which are the facts, which are the opinions? | **An Interview With …** Interview a character from the story. |
| Research | | |
| Criticise | | **This Is your Life** Write a biography for a character. |

# *Synthesis*

This level of thinking involves the use of old ideas to create new ones. It requires learners to predict and draw conclusions. It tests the learner's ability to be creative and unique.

| Key Words and Skills for this Level | Phrases to Assess Understanding at this Level | Tasks |
|---|---|---|
| Design | Devise a plan to test … | **Take Two**<br>Change a character's traits and rewrite a scene to reflect this change. |
| Rearrange | Propose an alternative solution to … | |
| Plan | | **If Only …**<br>Write a different ending to the story. |
| Prepare | Compose a … to show how … | |
| Create | Speculate on … | **Introducing**<br>Introduce another character to the story. |
| Rewrite | Plan an alternative course of action. | |
| Compose | Compose a … to promote … | **A Poem**<br>Write a poem about some aspect of the story. |
| Assemble | Can you devise a way to … ? | |
| Invent | Can you create a new way of … ? | **Story Props and Models**<br>Construct a model of an item from the story. |
| Present | Create a product that would enable … to … | |
| Devise | | **Dear Diary**<br>Keep a diary for a character for a day. |
| Formulate | Design a … that would enable … | |
| Organise | What would happen if … ? | **A Song**<br>Compose a song about an aspect of a story |
| Develop | Invent a … to do … | |
| Produce | Design a … for … | **Who's Next Door?**<br>Form an opinion about a character. |
| Choose | Design an experiment to test … | |
| Improve | | **A Picture Says a Thousand Words**<br>Create an illustration of the setting, a character or the plot. |
| Build | | |
| | | **Presenting …**<br>Create a multimedia presentation. |

 #HB-9653 © 2003 Hawker Brownlow Education

# *Evaluation*

This level of thinking involves judging the value of the information presented. It requires learners to develop and apply standards and criteria when evaluating information, ideas and materials. It tests the learner's ability to make sound choices after reviewing evidence.

| Key Words and Skills for this Level | Phrases to Assess Understanding at this Level | Tasks |
|---|---|---|
| Assess | Which is more logical, … or … ? Why do you think so? | **You Win Some, You Lose Some** List exciting and boring parts of the story. |
| Summarise | | |
| Test | Compare and contrast … | |
| Judge | Are there inconsistencies in … ? | **You Be the Judge** Write a list of criteria that could be used when judging the 'Book of the Year'. |
| Explain | Does the … follow a logical sequence? | |
| Support | | |
| Measure | Can you find errors in … ? | **For and Against** Focus on an issue from the story that will form the basis of a debate. |
| Select | Which … is better? | |
| Choose | | |
| Conclude | Determine … point of view. How effective is it? | **Everybody Wants to Be a Critic** Prepare a review of the story. |
| Recommend | Assess the value of … | **Character of the Week** Create an award for a good character. |
| Decide | | |
| Rank | Is the … subjective or objective? How can you tell? | |
| Justify | | **Book Cards** Make a display of books for the library or other public place. |
| Compare | Compare and discriminate between … | |
| Debate | | |
| Reject | Can you find the supporting argument in … ? | **What Would it Be Like?** What would it be like to be in the story you have just read? |
| Appraise | What do you think would happen if … ? | |
| Evaluate | | **What's the Point?** Determine the theme of a story. |
| Verify | Can you argue the opposite view to …? | |
| Convince | | **Picture This!** Paint or draw a particular aspect of the story. |
| Critique | Can you recommend a solution to …? | |
| Relate | | **Ratings** Rate aspects of the story based on a set of criteria. |
| Consider | Prepare a case for and against … | |

# Thinking Levels in Literature Tasks

## Bloom's Levels of Thinking in a Literature Context

### Knowledge

List all the characters in the story. Beside each name, record words from the text that the author used to describe each character.

### Comprehension

Explain how the young platypuses were taught to find food by their father.

### Evaluation

Write a letter to the man who captured Shy stating your reasons why he should not keep her for a pet.

### Shy the Platypus

an Aussie classic
by Leslie Rees

### Synthesis

Write a story based on the adventures of Shy's children.

### Application

Make a diorama of a scene from the story. Write a brief explanation of the scene and attach it to your diorama.

### Analysis

Describe the relationship between Shy and her mother.

# Thinking Levels in Integrated Units

## *Bloom's Levels of Thinking in an Integrated Curriculum Unit of Work*

**Knowledge**

Make a list of endangered animals and the country they are found in.

**Evaluation**

What might happen to human survival if all animals became extinct?

**Comprehension**

Choose an endangered animal and explain why it risks becoming extinct.

## Endangered Species

**Synthesis**

Create a badge with a logo that could be sold to generate funds for an endangered species.

**Application**

Write an article for your local paper explaining how people can help protect endangered animals to prevent them from becoming extinct.

**Analysis**

Choose four endangered animals. Construct a chart to show similarities and differences in the needs of these animals if they are to survive.

# *Classroom Organisation*

As the students will be required to accept some responsibility within the scope of the reading program, it becomes important to establish a routine that all students can follow. It is impossible to timetable all student activities; however, if the routine is the same for all students then the literacy block will run more efficiently and effectively. A system can be organised and planned by the classroom teacher along with student input and can be altered and adjusted until a workable procedure is in place.

# Program Outline

The tasks presented in this book incorporate all six levels of Bloom's cognitive domain. They encourage students to interact meaningfully with a variety of texts and to give more thought to the elements of story structure. The organisation of these tasks is left to the teacher's discretion and can easily be integrated into an existing classroom literacy program. A reading inventory (see page 91 for a template) can be given to students at the beginning of the year to ascertain their level of interest and their knowledge about books, authors and illustrators.

---

### *Reading Inventory*

Name ___ Jaimee McDougall ___

**What kind of books do you like to read?**
I like chapter books and picture books that are funny.

**Who are your favourite authors?**
Roald Dahl and I like Margaret Clark as well

**Who are your favourite illustrators?**
Graeme Base

**Which are your favourite books?**
The Twits by Roald Dahl and Pop by Margaret Clark

**List two books you have read recently.**

**Do you like to read? (Why? Why not?)**
Yes because I like to learn about a variety of things. I also like to read funny books because they make me laugh.

**Do you have any books of your own at home?**
Yes! Heaps

**Do you ever borrow books from the local library?**
Sometimes

---

The independent reading program outlined is designed to give students choice in what they read and how they respond to it. The program allows students to work at their own pace and level of ability while encouraging them to use thinking skills beyond the literal level.

As the students will be required to accept some responsibility within the scope of the reading program, it becomes important to establish a routine that all students can follow. It is impossible to timetable all student activities; however, if the routine is the same for all students then the literacy block will run more efficiently and effectively. A system can be organised and planned by the classroom teacher along with student input and can be altered and adjusted until a workable procedure is in place.

The following is an example of a procedure that can be used in a one-hour reading session.

# *Engaging*

The reading session begins with a teacher-prepared activity. The activity should focus on introducing children to a variety of texts written in different genres and styles. Discussion will usually follow the reading of the text. The discussion will involve students in learning about the elements of story structure, for example plot, characterisation, theme, setting and so on. Another appropriate activity would be to introduce an author or illustrator for an in-depth study. This is also an excellent time to introduce Bloom's levels of thinking, with one or two levels being introduced each week.

Some examples of introductory activities include:

- teaching children how to choose appropriate reading material
- discussing how the author builds anticipation and tension
- innovating on the text: for example changing the ending or beginning, adding a character, changing the traits of the main character or changing the setting
- modelling the processes of identifying main ideas, summarising, identifying keywords and phrases, story mapping and so on
- teaching children how to use a data chart as a means of recording information
- classifying characters according to similar or contrasting traits
- beginning an 'Our Favourite Books' list and adding to it throughout the year (Other lists could include favourite illustrators, authors, characters, story starters and so on.)
- creating a drawn story quilt with every child contributing a scene from the story (Variations could include collages or sewn scenes.)
- explaining how to prepare for a conference
- discussing links between text and illustrations.

# *Responding*

In the second part of the reading session, the students are involved in independent and small-group reading tasks, conferences and literature groups (the teaching group). The teacher's role is to guide and support the learners in their interactions with the texts and the follow-up activities. The teaching group sees the teacher's role shift from facilitator to teacher of specific reading skills.

During this time a number of activities could be happening simultaneously.

## Conferences

Some students may be involved in individual book conferences. After reading a text the student 'books in' for a conference. The student then meets with the teacher to explore the ideas and vocabulary of the text further. This should only take a few minutes. Prior to the conference the student prepares by making sure their reading journal is up to date and that they have completed their written comments about the book they have read.

The student comes to the conference with their reading journal and the book they have read. During the conference, the student discusses the written response and reads aloud a section of the story. The teacher listens, and responds by asking further questions. Again, questions based on Bloom's levels of thinking can be asked to ascertain the student's level of understanding. The main purpose of the conference is to gauge the student's comprehension of the text and to draw out their understanding of character and plot development, setting, mood, style and theme.

The teacher makes notes throughout the conference, noting strengths and areas of weaknesses that can be addressed during a teaching group session, used to report to parents and used to demonstrate ongoing progress during the year. The session will end with the student deciding whether to begin an activity or move on to a new text.

---

## Reading Journal

Name _Michael McDougall_

**Book Details**

Title _Harry Potter and the chamber of secrets_

Author _J. K. Rowling_

Illustrator (where applicable): _____

Genre _Fantasy_

I started reading this book on _13-8-02_

I finished reading this book on _10-9-02_

My Thoughts on this Book:

_Harry Potter and the chamber of secrets is about Harry trying to escape from Tom Riddle and the Basilisk who was sent to petrify all the muggle borns in the school. Luckily Harry, Ron and Hermione come to the rescue. My favourite part was when Harry and Ron were following the spiders into the dark forest. The spiders led Harry and Ron to Aragog who was a huge spider and they almost got eaten alive. It was very hard for me to put this book down once I started reading because I wanted to know how J. K. Rowling was going to reveal the end._

**Work Requirements** (Fill this in during the conference with your teachers.)

The activity I choose to do on this book is:

_____

## Literature Groups

A literature group consists of around six to eight children with common needs and similar abilities. The group meets each week and discusses a text the teacher has selected. The text may be a novel, a picture book, a factual text or another form of media, such as a newspaper article, that is linked to an integrated curriculum topic. It is important that there are multiple copies available so that each student has their own copy of the text.

During these sessions, the teacher's role is to teach reading skills and strategies that will assist students in interpreting and assimilating the information they read and help them become more efficient readers. These skills can be taught through a combination of guided and reciprocal reading or though more explicit lessons.

These sessions should include activities that teach:

• word recognition skills such as sight vocabulary and structural analysis (prefixes and suffixes, root words and so on)

• comprehension skills such as main idea, significant details, sequence of events, drawing conclusions, critical reading and vocabulary development

• the use of dictionaries and other reference materials such as Internet sites, encyclopedias, atlases, newspapers, reading tables, diagrams and graphs

• ways of predicting, confirming and integrating the reading cues – semantic, syntactic and graphophonic

• research skills, including interviews, taking notes, summarising, writing paragraphs, compiling bibliographies and proofreading.

Following the reading and discussion of the text, the teacher distributes an activity that focuses on one of the skills mentioned above. The students must complete and hand in the work prior to their next session. This gives the teacher time to respond to each completed task and plan a follow-up activity where necessary.

Unlike the individual conferences that only last a few minutes, the literature group usually meets for 20 to 30 minutes while the rest of the class is preparing for conferences or literature groups, or working on independent reading tasks.

## Independent Reading Tasks

The reading tasks presented in this book are another way of encouraging student responses to a story. They cover the six levels of Bloom's taxonomy: knowledge, comprehension, application, analysis, synthesis and evaluation. They also cover a variety of story structure elements such as character and plot analysis, setting, theme, mood, style, genre, illustrations and research on authors.

The teacher's role is to assist the students to select the most appropriate follow-up activity. It may come from any of the six levels, although it may be better to begin with one of the lower levels if embarking on this process for the first time. The teacher can then gradually introduce tasks from the higher-order thinking levels.

It is important to note that students do not have to complete a task for each book they read.

It may be that they prefer to read another story written by the same author or a story in the same genre. This should be encouraged. However, students are still required to make notes in their reading journal and attend a conference with the teacher for every text they read. This is important as it forms part of the teacher's evaluation of the student's understanding of the text.

# *Presenting*

The session concludes with students sharing their responses with other members of the class. Students may also have the opportunity at some other time to present to a wider audience such as another class or a school assembly.

Allowing children to present their completed tasks to an audience:

- promotes confidence in public speaking
- provides an opportunity to develop skills in responding to questions
- gives the audience a chance to see a completed task
- allows the audience to provide constructive criticism and commendations
- provides the audience with another opportunity to learn about aspects of story structure
- introduces texts that the audience may not know of.

When the student has finished their presentation the completed task can either be placed in their portfolio or put on display in the classroom, corridor, library, entrance foyer or the local shopping centre.

If the task was a play or a reading of the story, the students involved could video their performance and organise a time to perform in another classroom or at a school assembly.

# Materials

Many of the materials needed to complete these tasks are already available in schools. Teachers will need to set up a 'publishing centre' prior to beginning this program and then add to it during the year. Sending a letter home at the beginning of each term asking parents for bits and pieces may also be an option. It is crucial to the program to have a variety of materials on hand; for a child wanting to work on an activity, it is frustrating not to have the materials needed to complete the task.

### Proformas

- story map
- story board

### Computer Equipment

- *Kid Pix*
- *Hyperstudio*
- *Powerpoint*
- a word-processing program
- *Inspiration* or *Kidspiration*
- *Publisher*
- Internet access
- a scanner

### Other

- a felt board
- percussion instruments
- a digital camera
- a video camera

### Websites

- http://www.puzzlemaker.com
- http://www.teachingideas.co.uk/timefiller/magicpens.htm

### Craft Materials

- cardboard in a variety of sizes and colours
- felt pieces
- goggle eyes
- magazines and newspapers
- glitter
- coloured pencils, pastels, crayons, felt-tipped pens and so on
- paint
- cover paper – A3 and A4 in assorted colours
- threads and material
- modroc, plaster, clay, playdough, plasticine and so on
- bits and pieces to make puppets, models and dioramas

# *Worksheets*

**3**

Part three contains 60 independent reading tasks, ten for each level of Bloom's cognitive domain. The tasks require the students to think about aspects of story structure. Many of the tasks within the program incorporate information communication technologies. Students are encouraged to use a number of multimedia tools to publish their responses to the texts. The tasks also promote the use of online learning with opportunities for children to explore the Internet for relevant sites to assist them in their literature pursuits.

# Readers' Theatre

1. From a book you have just read, choose a scene or chapter that you think would make a good oral reading.

2. Ask some of your friends to participate in the presentation. Give them each a part to read aloud. Are there multiple copies of the book? If not, you may need to make a copy of the part to be read aloud for each person in your group.

3. Practise reading aloud with your friends. When everyone in the group is feeling confident, arrange a time when you could perform the play for your classmates or another grade in the school.

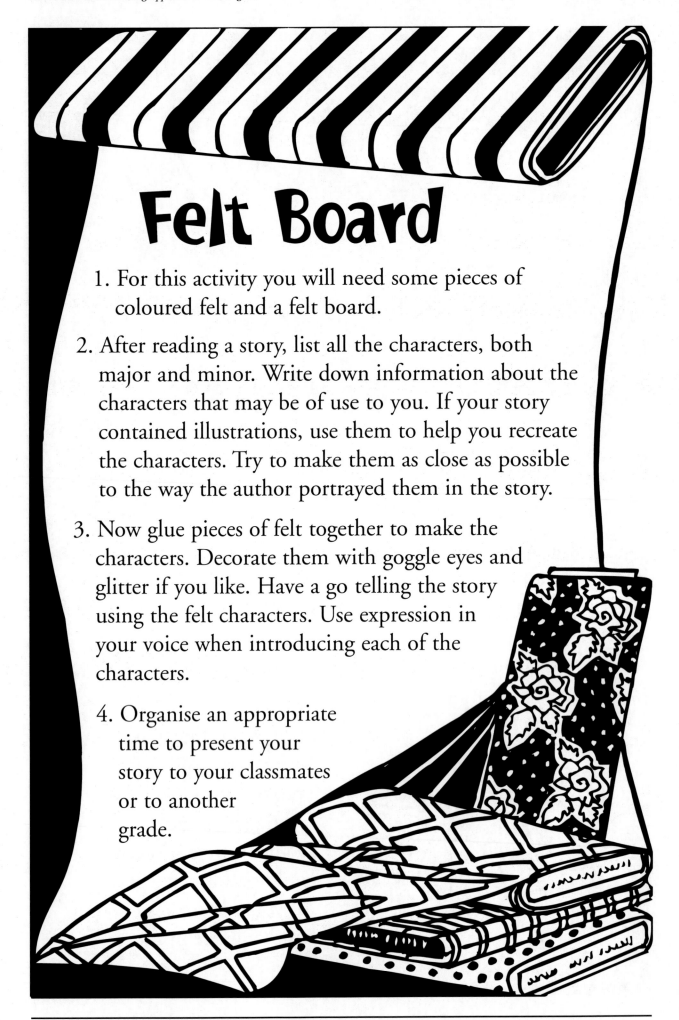

# Felt Board

1. For this activity you will need some pieces of coloured felt and a felt board.

2. After reading a story, list all the characters, both major and minor. Write down information about the characters that may be of use to you. If your story contained illustrations, use them to help you recreate the characters. Try to make them as close as possible to the way the author portrayed them in the story.

3. Now glue pieces of felt together to make the characters. Decorate them with goggle eyes and glitter if you like. Have a go telling the story using the felt characters. Use expression in your voice when introducing each of the characters.

4. Organise an appropriate time to present your story to your classmates or to another grade.

# Postcard

1. Select a passage describing a setting from a story you have just read.

2. On the front of a postcard-sized piece of cardboard, draw your interpretation of the setting from the text. You can use any form of media to decorate your card.

3. Consider using a drawing program like *Kid Pix* or *Hyperstudio* to create the setting. You can then print it out in colour, cut it to size and glue it on the front of your postcard.

4. On the other side of the postcard, write to someone telling them about the setting. Try writing a rough draft first. Check your spelling and punctuation. Now write it neatly on the back of the postcard.

 #HB-9653 © 2003 Hawker Brownlow Education

# Slide Show

1. For this activity you can use *Kid Pix*, *Hyperstudio* or *Powerpoint* to create a slide show of a book you have read.

2. First you will need to make a plan. What will your slide show look like? What information are you going to include? How many slides are you going to have?

3. Here are some ideas. You might like to include these in your slide show:

    • a retelling of the story with illustrations
    • a description of the characters in the story
    • a description of the setting
    • scanned pictures from the book.

4. When you have finished planning each slide, proofread your work carefully. Check the spelling and punctuation. Make sure it all makes sense and flows smoothly from one slide to the next.

# Story Map

1. List the events in a story you have just read. Make sure you list the events in the order in which they occurred.

2. Plan a draft map of the events. This could be illustrated. Begin with the very first event or perhaps the place where the first event occurred.

3. Continue mapping the events and settings.

4. When you have finished your rough draft, check that you have included sufficient details of the story and the setting. Begin your good copy.

5. You might like to illustrate your story map on coloured paper or use a drawing program like *Kid Pix*, *Hyperstudio* or *Paint*.

# Storyteller

1. Choose a picture storybook suitable for a younger audience. The text should contain simple language and ideas. The illustrations should be bold and help tell the story. Your teacher or school librarian may be able to help you with suitable titles. Another option would be to speak with the children's librarian at your local library.

2. Practise reading the story aloud with expression. If there are several characters in the story, create a different voice for each one.

3. When you feel confident, practise reading the story aloud to a friend or a group of your friends. Ask for constructive feedback. Keep reading aloud until you can read the book fluently and with expression.

4. Finally, arrange to read the story to a younger class, either at your school or at another local primary school. You might want to approach the local preschool as well. At the end of the story you might like to discuss aspects of the text with your audience or prepare some follow-up activities for them to complete.

# Word Puzzles

1. In this activity you will use words from a story to create a word puzzle. You can make your own word puzzle or you can go to <http://www.puzzlemaker.com>. This site has a number of word puzzles to choose from. You can type the words in and the program will create a puzzle for you.

2. First, decide on a theme for your puzzle. Here are some examples for you to choose from (or you can make up your own):
   • words about the setting
   • words about the characters
   • the different ways the author wrote 'said'
   • verbs, nouns, adverbs and adjectives
   • words from a particular scene.

3. Make a list of about fifteen to twenty words. If you decide to make your own crossword puzzle you will need to provide the clues. If you create a word search make sure you list the words that need to be found.

4. When you have completed the puzzle give it to one of your friends to do.

# Bookmark

1. After reading a story, select a scene or a character from the book to illustrate on the front of a bookmark.

2. Next, decide on the shape of your bookmark. Most are rectangular but you can decide on any shape. For instance, if the story you read was about a cat, you might like to make your bookmark in a shape of a cat.

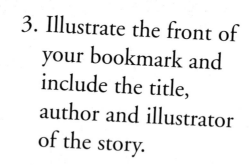

3. Illustrate the front of your bookmark and include the title, author and illustrator of the story.

4. On the back of your bookmark write a blurb about the story. Proofread your writing carefully!

# Story Poster

1. Think about a poster you could create from the story you have just read. Think about how you want it to look and brainstorm different layouts on rough paper. Where will you position the text and illustrations?

2. Your poster should include as much information about the book as possible. You will need to include details about the plot, setting, characters and your favourite scene in the story. Write a rough draft and then proofread it. Show your draft to your teacher.

3. Consider where you will position the title of the story, as well as the names of the author and illustrator. What type of lettering will you use? Will you use paint, pencils, textas, pastels, crayons or a drawing program such as *Kid Pix*? When you have planned the layout and corrected your draft, begin your good copy.

# Character Mobiles

1. Make a list of all the characters from a story you have read. Beside each name write a list of words that describe the character. These words can come from the text or from your understanding of the character.

2. On pieces of cardboard, draw pictures of the characters. Make each one at least 15 centimetres tall. If your book had illustrations you could use them to help you with your drawings. Colour in each character and cut around the outline of each one.

3. On the bottom of each character attach a paragraph or list of words describing each character's traits.

4. Assemble your characters with string and hang them from pieces of dowel or a coathanger.

5. Find a suitable place to hang your mobile. Maybe there's a spot for it in the library.

# WHO'S WHO

1. In this activity you will be comparing and contrasting two characters from the same story.

2. You will need an A3-sized reproduction of a Venn diagram for your good copy.

3. On a piece of paper, rule three columns. At the top of the first column, write the first character's name. At the top of the third column, write the second character's name. In the middle column write the names of both characters.

4. In the first column write down all the traits specific to that character only. Do the same in the third column for the second character. In the middle column write down all the traits shared by both characters.

5. Proofread your work. Make sure there are no spelling errors. Now you are ready to begin your good copy on the Venn diagram. Your columns have now become circles. The description of your first character goes in the first circle, the other character in the second circle. The similarities go in the area where the circles overlap. Make sure your writing is neat and legible.

6. Decorate your page with drawings of the characters and scenes from the story.

# TALKFEST

1. Choose two characters from a story you have read. Write down a brief description of what these characters are like. For example fair, bossy, kind, mean or friendly.

2. Create a scene for the two characters, for instance an accident, a nasty incident or an argument over the last lolly. Given what these characters are like, think about what they would say to one another.

3. Now draw these characters having a conversation with each other. Their conversation should reflect the traits of each character as portrayed by the author of the story.

4. You might like to enclose your characters' conversation inside a speech bubble or write a script if their conversation is a particularly long one.

# LIFT THE FLAP

1. For this activity you need to construct a 'lift the flap' chart. You will need two pieces of A3 cover paper. On one piece, rule five columns from top to bottom. Glue the top part of this piece of paper onto the top of the second piece. Cut along the lines on the top piece, stopping when you reach the part that you glued down.

2. In the first column on the top piece of paper, write down the title, author and illustrator of the book you have read. Underneath the 'flap' draw a scene from the story that reflects the title. Write a sentence explaining your drawing.

3. In the second column write the word 'Setting'. Underneath the flap draw a picture of the main setting in the story. Briefly describe it in your own words.

4. In the third column write the word 'Complication'. Underneath the flap write a brief explanation of what the problem was in the story. Draw a picture to help illustrate your explanation.

5. In the fourth column write 'Characters'. Write a brief description of the main character, stating why they were important to the story. Draw a picture of this character.

6. In the fifth column write 'Solution'. Write a brief statement on how the problem in the story was resolved. Was it, in your opinion, a satisfactory resolution? Why or why not?

# KEEPING TRACK

1. After reading a book, create a graphic organiser, for example a flowchart or a concept map, using a software package such as *Inspiration* or *Word*. Alternatively you can hand draw your own.

2. First, you will need to decide the content of your graphic organiser. For instance, do you want to show a sequence of events, the changes in the setting, or the relationship between the characters?

3. When you have decided, carefully jot down your ideas. What important information are you going to include? Does the information flow smoothly? Does it make sense? Have you included as much relevant information as possible?

4. Proofread your work carefully and then decorate your graphic organiser by inserting pictures from a file or your own illustrations based on the book.

# GAME TIME

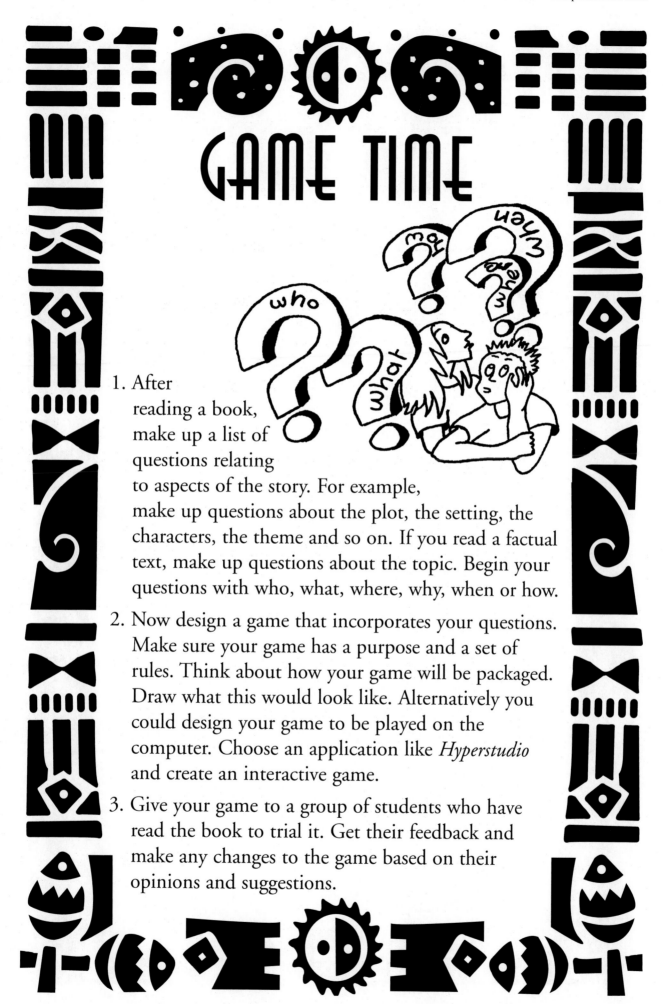

1. After reading a book, make up a list of questions relating to aspects of the story. For example, make up questions about the plot, the setting, the characters, the theme and so on. If you read a factual text, make up questions about the topic. Begin your questions with who, what, where, why, when or how.

2. Now design a game that incorporates your questions. Make sure your game has a purpose and a set of rules. Think about how your game will be packaged. Draw what this would look like. Alternatively you could design your game to be played on the computer. Choose an application like *Hyperstudio* and create an interactive game.

3. Give your game to a group of students who have read the book to trial it. Get their feedback and make any changes to the game based on their opinions and suggestions.

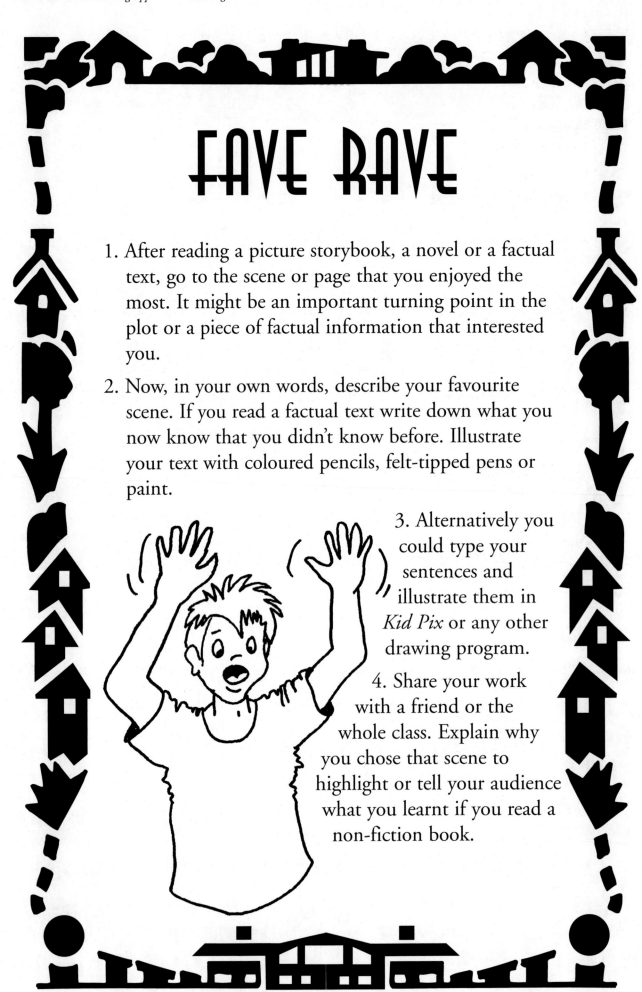

# FAVE RAVE

1. After reading a picture storybook, a novel or a factual text, go to the scene or page that you enjoyed the most. It might be an important turning point in the plot or a piece of factual information that interested you.

2. Now, in your own words, describe your favourite scene. If you read a factual text write down what you now know that you didn't know before. Illustrate your text with coloured pencils, felt-tipped pens or paint.

3. Alternatively you could type your sentences and illustrate them in *Kid Pix* or any other drawing program.

4. Share your work with a friend or the whole class. Explain why you chose that scene to highlight or tell your audience what you learnt if you read a non-fiction book.

# DESIGN A SET

1. Think about the setting of a story you have read. Write a detailed description of where the main part of the story takes place.

2. Using this description, make a list of props and sets that could be used in a stage performance of the story. Draw each item on your list.

3. Draw a plan showing how the sets and props are to be arranged on the stage. Label everything on your plan so that the people setting up the stage will know where everything goes.

4. Attach your description of the setting to your stage plan. If material is readily available you may want to make one of your props or background sets and submit it with your plan.

#HB-9653 © 2003 Hawker Brownlow Education

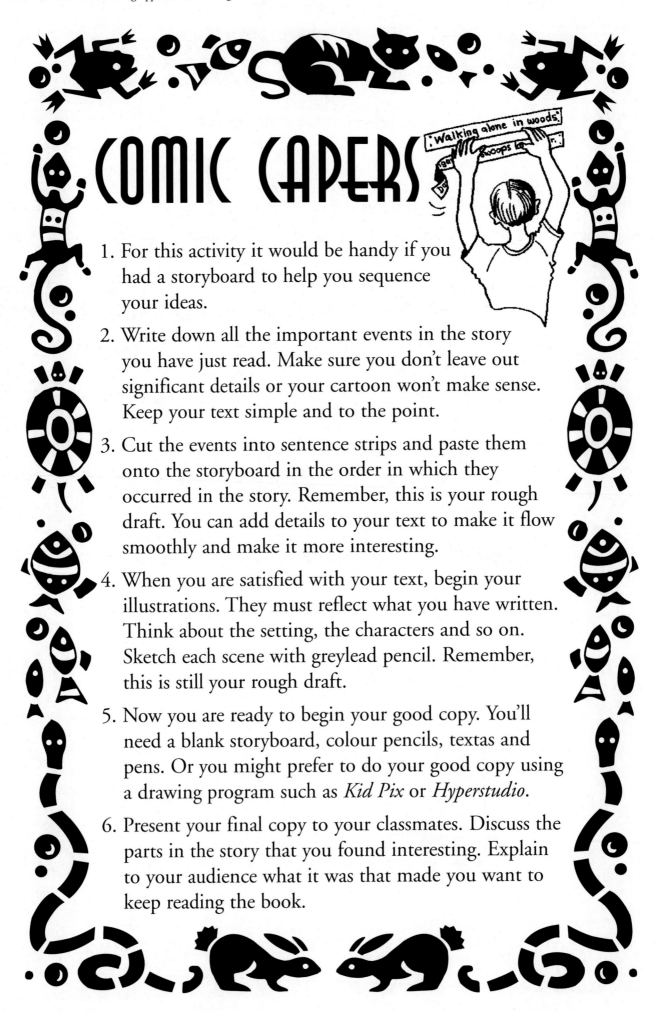

# COMIC CAPERS

1. For this activity it would be handy if you had a storyboard to help you sequence your ideas.

2. Write down all the important events in the story you have just read. Make sure you don't leave out significant details or your cartoon won't make sense. Keep your text simple and to the point.

3. Cut the events into sentence strips and paste them onto the storyboard in the order in which they occurred in the story. Remember, this is your rough draft. You can add details to your text to make it flow smoothly and make it more interesting.

4. When you are satisfied with your text, begin your illustrations. They must reflect what you have written. Think about the setting, the characters and so on. Sketch each scene with greylead pencil. Remember, this is still your rough draft.

5. Now you are ready to begin your good copy. You'll need a blank storyboard, colour pencils, textas and pens. Or you might prefer to do your good copy using a drawing program such as *Kid Pix* or *Hyperstudio*.

6. Present your final copy to your classmates. Discuss the parts in the story that you found interesting. Explain to your audience what it was that made you want to keep reading the book.

# CHARACTER TRAITS

1. Choose a character from a story you have read. It can be a character that has a major or a minor part in the story.

2. Make a list of words that accurately describes this character. For example, was this character nasty? Clever? Happy? Greedy? What did the character look like? Fair? Huge? Skinny? Pointy face? Large ears? Use the text from the book to assist you in this activity.

3. Now draw a picture of your character in something they would wear. Write your descriptive words inside or around the shape of your character.

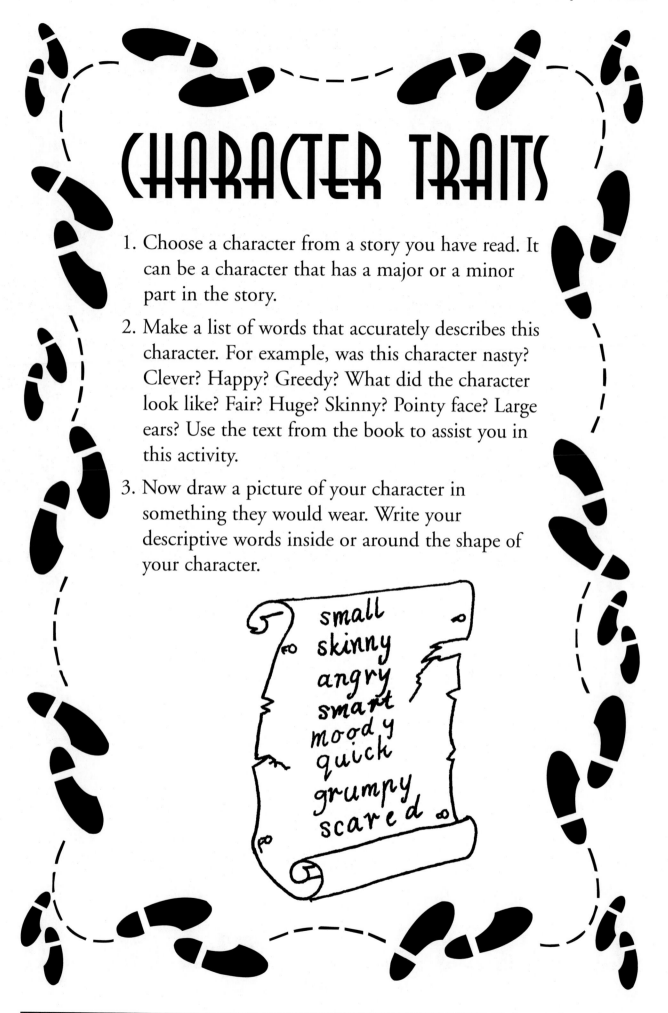

small
skinny
angry
smart
moody
quick
grumpy
scared

#HB-9653 © 2003 Hawker Brownlow Education

# ACTING UP!

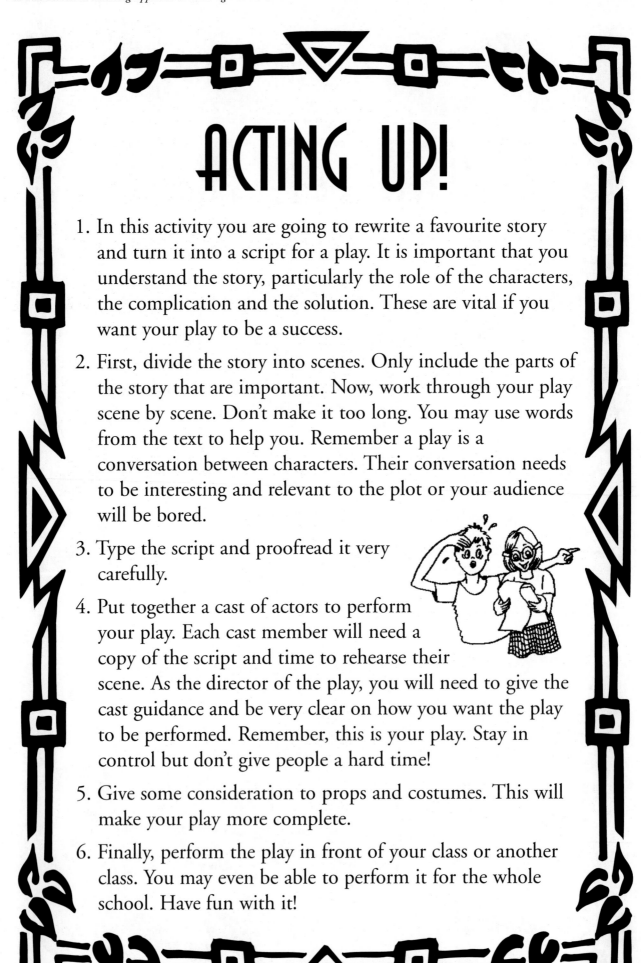

1. In this activity you are going to rewrite a favourite story and turn it into a script for a play. It is important that you understand the story, particularly the role of the characters, the complication and the solution. These are vital if you want your play to be a success.

2. First, divide the story into scenes. Only include the parts of the story that are important. Now, work through your play scene by scene. Don't make it too long. You may use words from the text to help you. Remember a play is a conversation between characters. Their conversation needs to be interesting and relevant to the plot or your audience will be bored.

3. Type the script and proofread it very carefully.

4. Put together a cast of actors to perform your play. Each cast member will need a copy of the script and time to rehearse their scene. As the director of the play, you will need to give the cast guidance and be very clear on how you want the play to be performed. Remember, this is your play. Stay in control but don't give people a hard time!

5. Give some consideration to props and costumes. This will make your play more complete.

6. Finally, perform the play in front of your class or another class. You may even be able to perform it for the whole school. Have fun with it!

# HOLIDAYS!

1. Get ready for the holiday of a lifetime! You are going to visit the place (the setting) in the story you have read. Consider and make a list of what you will pack in your suitcase. Be prepared to discuss your choices.

2. Now write yourself an itinerary. This is a plan of what you will see and do each day. Remember, you are visiting the place where the story was set. Think about the places you will visit and the people you might meet. For instance, there may be a castle you could explore or a wizard to visit.

3. When you have returned from your journey, present your 'photos' (pictures) or 'slides' (*PowerPoint* or *Kid Pix*) to your class. Talk about the places you visited in the story and the characters you met along the way.

# LET'S CELEBRATE

1. You have been given the task of organising a birthday party for the main character of the book you have just read.

2. First you will need to make a list of the people you are going to invite. Are there characters in the story you would consider inviting? Why or why not? Design the invitation cards.

3. Now think about the kind of games your character would like to play. Write a list of these. Don't forget to write down how you play these games.

4. Every party must have food. Plan the party menu. What food would your character like to have at the party?

5. Finally, choose a present for your character. What kind of present would they like? Why did you choose this particular present?

# ON THE SCENE REPORTER

1. Here's your chance to be a TV reporter! The subject of your report will be the story you have just finished reading. You will need to gather as many facts as you can about the story. Watch the news on TV to get ideas on how to present stories.

2. Start with the plot. Every story has a conflict. What was the problem the main character had to face in your story? Try to retell it as a news story. Make it as interesting as you can.

3. Another idea is to interview the main character and let them tell the story in their own words. Of course you will need to write the script for them!

4. When you have written your news story, show your teacher. He or she may be able to give you more ideas or help you with the wording.

5. Proofread your work carefully. Make sure there are no spelling mistakes.

6. Finally, ask someone to video you when you present your report. Remember to use your best news reporter's voice.

 #HB-9653 © 2003 Hawker Brownlow Education

# PLAYING GAMES

Many wonderful stories, both fiction and factual, have been made into games. For example, the *Titanic*, *Jumanji* and *Winnie the Pooh*, just to name a few. Now you can design and make a board game based on a story you have just read.

1. Make a list of all the games you have at home or that you have played with. Now, think about the games you enjoyed playing. Why were they so much fun?

2. Make a plan of what you want your game to look like. Include details such as layout, illustrations and rules. Will your game need cards, tokens or dice? Make a list of all the 'extras' you will need. Make sure your game reflects the story. Include information and illustrations about the characters, setting and plot. Try to retell the story or a scene from the story through your game.

3. When you're happy with your plan, show your teacher. He or she will discuss your game and make sure you have included everything you need to make your game a success.

4. Begin your good copy. You may want to use the computer or hand-draw the game. Make sure your writing is neat and without spelling errors and that your game is colourful and eye-catching.

5. Choose some friends to play the game with you. Have fun with it! You could lend your game to another class to play with it too.

# PUPPET SHOW

1. A puppet show gives you the opportunity to retell a story you have read to an audience. First, make a list of all the characters in the story. Write a brief description about each one. What are their personalities like? What do they look like?

2. Now decide how you will make your puppets. Will you make them from papier-mache, paper or felt? Will they be stick puppets, finger puppets or glove puppets? When you have decided, you will need to collect all the materials required to make them.

3. You will need to write talking parts (a script) for your puppets. Make sure their part is true to the story and that it makes sense. Practise reading the parts of all your characters. Try using different voices and expressions.

4. Organise a time to perform your puppet show to an audience.

#HB-9653 © 2003 Hawker Brownlow Education

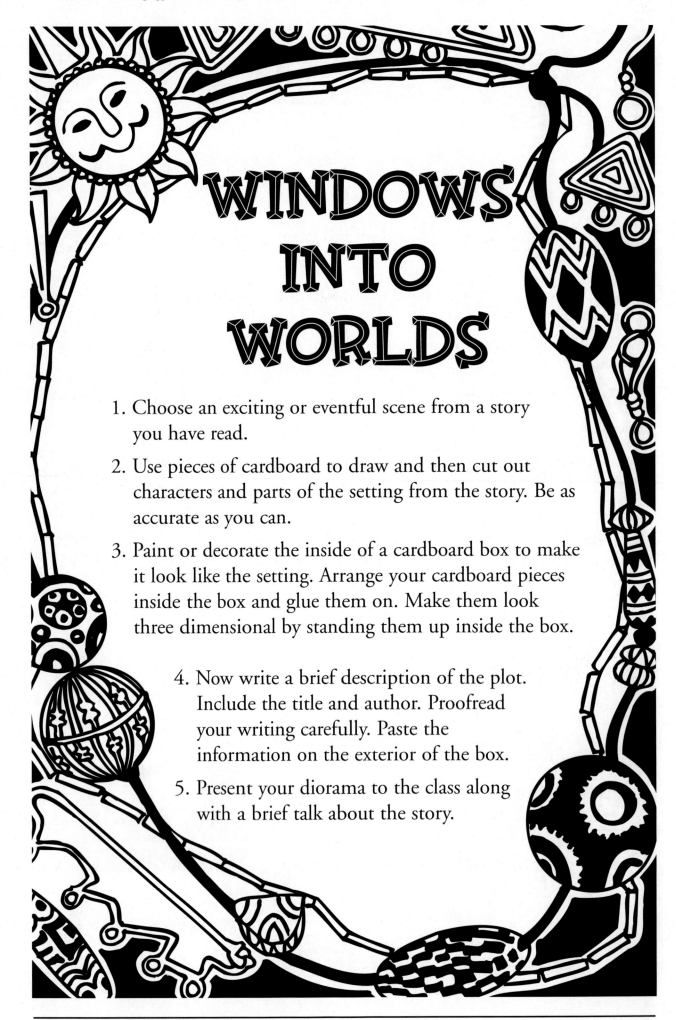

# WINDOWS INTO WORLDS

1. Choose an exciting or eventful scene from a story you have read.

2. Use pieces of cardboard to draw and then cut out characters and parts of the setting from the story. Be as accurate as you can.

3. Paint or decorate the inside of a cardboard box to make it look like the setting. Arrange your cardboard pieces inside the box and glue them on. Make them look three dimensional by standing them up inside the box.

4. Now write a brief description of the plot. Include the title and author. Proofread your writing carefully. Paste the information on the exterior of the box.

5. Present your diorama to the class along with a brief talk about the story.

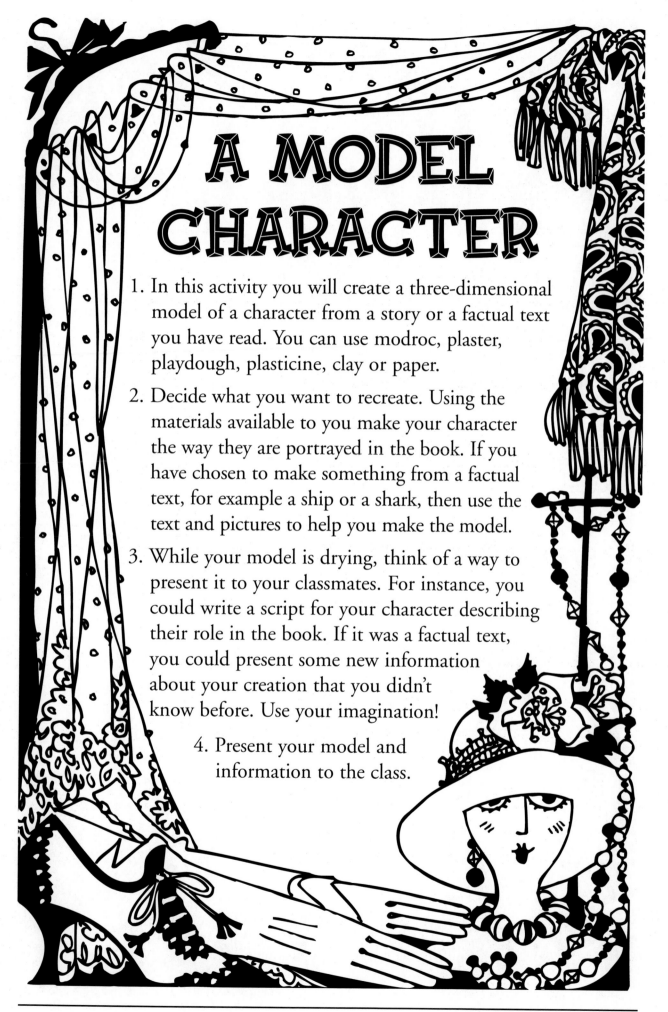

# A MODEL CHARACTER

1. In this activity you will create a three-dimensional model of a character from a story or a factual text you have read. You can use modroc, plaster, playdough, plasticine, clay or paper.

2. Decide what you want to recreate. Using the materials available to you make your character the way they are portrayed in the book. If you have chosen to make something from a factual text, for example a ship or a shark, then use the text and pictures to help you make the model.

3. While your model is drying, think of a way to present it to your classmates. For instance, you could write a script for your character describing their role in the book. If it was a factual text, you could present some new information about your creation that you didn't know before. Use your imagination!

4. Present your model and information to the class.

#HB-9653 © 2003 Hawker Brownlow Education

# COVER UP!

1. This activity requires you to make a dust jacket for a book you have read.

2. You will need plain or coloured cover paper. Measure the paper and cut it to size. Make sure you leave enough for the flaps.

3. Draw the cover on the front page. Be sure to include such information as title and author. Draw a picture of a scene from the story.

4. On the front flap, write a blurb about the story. Write it so others will want to read it.

5. On the back flap write a brief biography of the author. Include information on other books this person has written. If the book had an illustrator, try to find information about him or her as well. Try getting the information from the Internet. Sometimes well-known authors and illustrators have their own webpage.

6. On the back cover write your opinion of the story. What did you like or not like about the story? Who was your favourite or least favourite character? Be creative in your response!

7. Place the dust jacket over the book and put it on display somewhere prominent.

# STORY STARTERS

1. The opening lines of a story are crucial. The author needs to 'grab' the reader's attention and maintain their interest.

2. Write out the first few opening sentences of a story you were 'glued' to. What was it that made you want to continue reading? Underline the words that grabbed your attention.

3. Think of an interesting way to begin a story. Write it down on a file card and place it in a 'Super File of Writing Ideas' box. The website below will give you some ideas:

   Magic Pen Starters
   http://www.teachingideas.co.uk/timefiller/magicpens.htm

4. Do a search for similar sites.

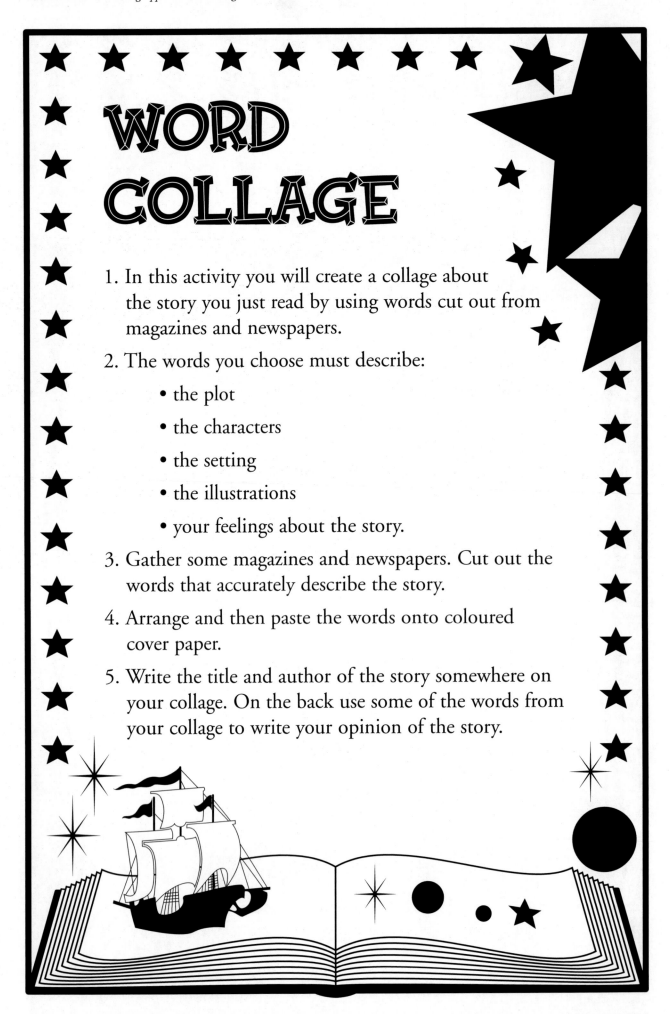

# WORD COLLAGE

1. In this activity you will create a collage about the story you just read by using words cut out from magazines and newspapers.

2. The words you choose must describe:

   • the plot

   • the characters

   • the setting

   • the illustrations

   • your feelings about the story.

3. Gather some magazines and newspapers. Cut out the words that accurately describe the story.

4. Arrange and then paste the words onto coloured cover paper.

5. Write the title and author of the story somewhere on your collage. On the back use some of the words from your collage to write your opinion of the story.

# WHAT ARE THEY REALLY LIKE?

1. From a story you have just read, select one of the main characters.

2. Compile an A to Z list of words to describe the character you have selected. For example A – active, B – brave and so on.

3. Now proofread your work. Make sure there are no spelling errors.

4. Decide how you want to present your final copy. For example, you could design a poster or a slide show using *PowerPoint*, *Kid Pix* or *Hyperstudio*.

5. When you have finished, share the final product with your classmates. Give a brief outline of the story and discuss the role of the character.

# WANTED!

1. Was there a character you didn't like in the story you have just read? Here's your chance to unveil the dark side of this character. You are going to create a 'Wanted' poster.

2. First, list the characteristics of the character that made them evil, unkind or naughty. Use these characteristics to write a statement for your poster. Think of a catchy heading; for example 'Evil Wizard Wanted for the Illegal Imprisonment of Princess Fairweather'. Don't forget to proofread your text.

3. Now draw a portrait of your character. Make them look mean or cheeky depending on their characteristics. Colour your portrait with pencils, charcoal, pastels or paint.

4. You may prefer to create your poster in *Publisher* or *Word*. You could scan your portrait and insert it into your design.

5. Present your Wanted poster to your class. Give a description of your character. Display your work in the 'Rogues Gallery'.

# UNDER THE MICROSCOPE

1. Using the program *Word*, create a three-column table. Label the first column 'Plus', the second column 'Minus' and the last column 'Interesting'.

2. In the 'Plus' column, list all the positive or good things about a story you have read. Think about things that made the story appealing and made you want to read on. List the exciting parts.

3. In the 'Minus' column, list all the negative or bad things about the story. What parts were boring? Which scenes could you have easily skimmed through?

4. In the 'Interesting' column, list all the aspects of the story you found interesting.

5. Proofread your work for spelling errors. Check that it makes sense.

6. Finally, discuss your 'Plus, Minus, Interesting' table with your teacher. Be prepared to justify your responses.

# STEP RIGHT UP!

1. In this activity, you will create an advertisement to promote a story you like. Your ad can be written for television, for radio, for a billboard or for a magazine.

2. Remember, the aim of your ad is to promote the story in as few words as possible. Your text and illustrations should arouse buyers' interest and make them want to read the book.

3. Brainstorm possible slogans or jingles with a friend or your teacher. Try your hand at a variety of illustrations that reflect an exciting aspect of the story.

4. Now decide how you want to present your ad. You could use paper or a program such as *Publisher* to create a poster, or a multimedia application such as *PowerPoint*, *Hyperstudio* or *Kid Pix* to design an ad for television. You could even use a cassette recorder to tape your ad for radio. Don't forget to proofread your work!

5. You are now ready to present your designs to your classmates. You might even like to show them a copy of the book and read excerpts from it.

# MAYBE ... MAYBE NOT ...

1. After reading a story, think very carefully about the plot, setting and characters.

2. Open up a *Word* document and create a two-column table. Label one column 'Maybe' and the other 'Maybe Not'.

3. In the column titled 'Maybe', list all the events in the story that could occur in real life. Could there be a setting like the one described in the story? Could characters like these really exist? Were there events that could really take place? Think carefully about your responses.

4. In the column titled 'Maybe Not', list all the events in the story that you think couldn't possibly happen in real life. Are there aspects of the plot that just don't ring true? Do the characters display traits that are too unbelievable? Is the setting based in a fantasy world? Again, think carefully about your responses.

5. Proofread your work carefully and then present your information to your teacher. Be prepared to explain the reasoning behind your choices.

# I WONDER WHAT WOULD HAPPEN IF ...

1. Every narrative has a conflict or problem. Identify the problem in a story you have read.

2. Now write four other possible solutions to the problem. They must be believable and in keeping with the overall story-line.

3. Now create a table in *Word* that contains four squares (that is, two columns and two rows). After proofreading your endings, type each one inside the squares of the table.

4. Discuss your work with your teacher. Explain which solution you liked the best and why. Be prepared to justify your choice. How is it different to the original solution presented in the story?

# DEAR AUTHOR

1. In this activity you will have the opportunity to write to the author of a story you have read giving them your opinion of the story.

2. In your letter you could discuss certain aspects of the story, for example:
   • the way the author treated the characters
   • how the author kept you interested in the story
   • the ending of the story; could you suggest a different ending?
   • was there enough information or too much?
   • a comparison with other books the author has written
   • whether the illustrations suited the story.
   These are only suggestions; you may have other ideas!

3. When you have finished your letter, carefully proofread it. Show your teacher. Decide on a format; you may be able to email your letter. Check the Internet – your author may have their own website with an email address. If not, try sending your letter by email or snail mail to the author's publisher. They can then pass it on. Good luck!

# BACK TO THE PAST

1. The year is 2101, one hundred years after the story you just read was written. Archaeologists have been digging around and discovered the setting where your story took place.

2. Write a description of what they discovered. Consider what would have survived 100 years and what would not have survived.

3. What relics would they have found that belonged to the characters? Draw a picture of what the archaeologists found. Label each item.

4. Make a 'Then and Now' comparison in a report based on your responses to steps 2 and 3.

5. Proofread your work and then decide how you want to present your final copy. Discuss some options with your friends or your teacher.

# AN INTERVIEW WITH ...

1. You are going to have the rare opportunity to interview a character from a story you have read.

2. First, write a list of possible questions you could ask this character. Make sure the questions are relevant to the story. The idea is to make the character reveal more about their thoughts and feelings.

3. Type the questions, leaving enough room for the responses. Make sure there are no spelling or grammatical errors.

4. Given what you know about the character, respond to each question the way you think your character would. Proofread your work; if you are using a computer, try using the spell check.

5. Show you final product to your teacher. She or he may have a few questions as well!

# THIS IS YOUR LIFE ...

1. In this activity you are going to write a biography about the main character of the story you have just read. A biography is a story about the life of a person.

2. Write down everything you can remember about the main character. You might need to re-read sections of the book.

3. Now begin writing about the life of the character based on your notes. Include such information as:
   - birthplace and birth date
   - hobbies or interests
   - major events in their life
   - family details
   - likes and dislikes
   - type of person they are
   - relationships with other characters
   - anything else you can think of.

4. When you have completed your biography, proofread it carefully. Decide on how you want to publish it. You could either hand-write it neatly or design an e-album using *PowerPoint*. Present your final copy to the class.

# Take Two

1. In this activity you are going to choose one of the characters from a story you have read and give them a complete change of personality.

2. When you have chosen your character, list their character traits as portrayed in the story. What kind of personality has the author given this character? Are they shy? Boisterous? A bully? Write down as many words as you can that describe them.

3. Now list words to describe your character's new personality. Remember, you are giving your character a complete personality change. If your character is timid, then you might make them brash and loud. A thesaurus may be of use if you are stuck for words.

4. Choose a scene from the story that your character is in and rewrite it. The new scene must reflect the change in the character's personality.

5. Draw a picture of the new scene. Include the text you wrote that reflects the change in your character.

6. Discuss your work with your teacher. Explain the changes you made and why you made them.

# If Only ...

1. In this activity you will be focusing on the ending of a story you have just read. Consider these questions:
   - Why do you think the author decided to end the story in this way?
   - Were you able to guess what was going to happen at the end?

2. You are going to write a different ending to the story. Your ending must still be in keeping with the original plot and it has to make sense.

3. Begin a rough draft. Make sure it is logical. Don't just introduce a new character or setting; it has to make sense.

4. Read over your draft. Discuss your work with your teacher. He or she might be able to give you a few extra hints.

5. When you are happy with the content, proofread your work for spelling and punctuation errors.

6. Present your ending to the class. You may need to give a brief synopsis of the story before you present the new ending. It might be possible to email the alternative ending to the author with reasons why you changed the ending the way you did.

# Introducing ...

1. Characters play a very important role in a story. They bring the story to life and give it some meaning. Make a list of the characters of a story you have read. Choose one character and explain why this character is important in the story.

2. You are going to introduce another character to the story. Think about the role this character will play:
   - At what point in the story are you going to introduce this character?
   - What impact will they have?
   - Will this character change the direction of the story or complement it in some way?

3. Decide at which point in the story you will introduce this character. How are the other characters going to react to this character?

4. Begin rewriting the original story with the new character added to it. Your story must flow smoothly and logically. Read your story to a classmate to see if it makes sense to them. Make a time to read it to your teacher.

5. When you are happy with the content, begin proofreading for spelling and punctuation errors.

6. Think about how you will publish your story. You might like to create an e-book (a digital book) or make a picture book. Whatever you decide, remember to have fun!

 #HB-9653 © 2003 Hawker Brownlow Education

# A Poem

1. In this activity you will be writing a poem about something to do with the story you have read. It may be about a character, the setting or something to do with the plot. The choice is yours.

2. There are many different styles of poetry. The following are examples that you might want to use, or you can make up your own. Remember, however, that the poem must be about an aspect of the story.

   • **Diamante**

   line 1: one noun
   line 2: two adjectives which describe the noun in the first line
   line 3: three words ending in 'ing' that describe the noun
   line 4: four nouns; two that are related to line 1 and two that are related to the last line
   line 5: three words ending in 'ing' that describe the last noun
   line 6: two adjectives that describe the last noun
   line 7: one noun that is different to the first noun

   • **Cinquain**

   line 1: a two-syllable word or words (the title)
   line 2: four syllables describing the title
   line 3: six syllables stating an action
   line 4: eight syllables expressing feelings
   line 5: two syllables which are a synonym for the title

   • **Acrostic**

   In this type of poem you start with the title, the name of a character or one word that describes the setting. The word is written vertically and then a word or sentence that relates to the story is written beside each letter.

3. You might like to illustrate your poem using pencils or a drawing program such as *Kid Pix*. Present your poem to the class along with a brief description of the story.

# Story Props and Models

1. In this activity you are going to construct a prop or model of an item from the story you have read. For example, you might make:
   - a model of a witch's broom
   - a wizard's wand
   - a king's castle
   - an alien spaceship.

2. Once you have decided what you are going to construct, gather the things you will need to make this model.

3. When you have completed your model, write a brief description of its relevance to the story on a card and attach it your model.

4. Present your model to the class, along with a brief explanation of the story.

# Dear Diary

1. For this activity you will need to step into the shoes of a character in a story and keep their diary for a day.

2. Before you begin writing, give some thought to the characteristics of this person. Are they:
   • good or bad?
   • a troublemaker or do-gooder?
   • sensible or thoughtless?
   • dependable or unreliable?
   • happy or sad?

3. Now choose a scene from the story and rewrite it in a diary format. Remember, you are writing from your character's point of view and therefore must write as they would.

4. Proofread your work and then begin your good copy. You might want to use a software program like *Amazing Writing Machine*. It has a diary format you could use, or you might want to write it out in your best handwriting.

5. Present your work to the class along with a brief description of your character and their role in the story.

# A Song

1. In this activity you will compose a song about a story you have read. It can be about any aspect of the story you like. Here are some ideas:
   - a character
   - the plot
   - the setting
   - the theme.

2. There are many music files on the Internet that you can access for this activity. Try doing a search. One option is to download the music and write your own lyrics. If you prefer, you could compose a song using a variety of percussion instruments.

3. Finally, get together a group of friends and perform the song at assembly or in front of your class. As an introduction you might like to give a brief explanation of the book.

 #HB-9653 © 2003 Hawker Brownlow Education

# Who's Next Door?

1. Imagine a character from a story you have read has moved in next door to your house. Give reasons why you would or wouldn't want to live next door to this person.

2. Think about how the character behaved in the story. It will help shape your response. Was the character:
   - a troublemaker?
   - helpful towards others?
   - kind and thoughtful?
   - mean and nasty?
   - sensible?
   - silly?

3. When you are sure of your feelings towards this person, begin writing either a welcome speech or a letter of protest depending on how you feel about your new neighbour.

4. Share your response with your classmates. Explain why you feel the way you do.

# A Picture Says a Thousand Words

1. For this activity you need to choose a passage that vividly describes the setting, a character or an interesting scene in a story you have read.

2. Once you have selected the part of the story you want to illustrate, you will need to think about how you will go about creating a picture that clearly shows your own interpretation of what you read. Will you present your ideas in:

   • an abstract painting?
   • a collage?
   • a photomontage?
   • a quilt?

3. When you have decided, begin your work of art. Your interpretation of the scene or character is what's important.

4. When you have completed your creation, present your work to the class. Explain the part of the story you have illustrated and why you chose to present it the way you did.

# Presenting ...

1. In this activity you will create either a *PowerPoint* or a *Hyperstudio* presentation on certain aspects of a story you have read.

2. You will need to prepare a plan of your presentation. It will need to include information on the following:
   - the author
   - other titles by the author
   - a brief description of the book and why you liked it
   - aspects of the story you would like to highlight
   - the characters and how each one contributes to the development of the plot
   - links to the author's webpage, if they have one.

3. When you have gathered all your information, begin your slide show. Don't forget to insert pictures, graphics and sound to accompany your text.

4. Present your slide show to your classmates, complete with a commentary and copies of other books written by the author.

# You Win Some, You Lose Some

1. Using *Word* or another word-processing program, create a table with two columns and about five rows.

2. Think about the story you have just read, then list all the episodes in the story that were exciting in the first column of your table. These are the parts of the story that made you want to read on because you wanted to find out what would happen next. Give reasons for your choices.

3. In the second column, list all the episodes in the story that were boring. These are the parts of the story that you wanted to skim over because they weren't very exciting. Once again, give reasons for your choices.

4. Proofread your work and present your final copy to your teacher and classmates. Explain to your audience why you think they should or should not read the book.

# You Be the Judge

1. You have been selected to be a member of a judging panel. This position requires you to write a list of criteria that could be used when judging the 'Book of the Year' competition.

2. Decide whether your criteria will be used to judge a picture storybook, a novel or a factual text; or you might like to set criteria for all three.

3. Set a limit of five criteria for each category you choose. Remember, the criteria will be used to shortlist a number of books in each category. Think about the questions you'll need to ask yourself when judging a book. Consider such things as the plot, how the characters evolve through the story, the illustrations (if it's a picture book) and the theme.

4. When you have written your criteria, show your teacher. Proofread your work together.

5. Invite classmates to use your criteria to select a book for the short-listing process. Set up a panel of judges. The panel's role is to select the 'Book of the Year' from all the entries. Again, use the same criteria for consistency. Narrow the choice to one book by discussing and comparing choices with the other panel members.

6. Present the final choice to the class along with the reasons why the book won the 'Book of the Year' award. Design an award certificate and send it to the author with the reasons why their book won the award.

# For and Against

1. For this activity you will be focusing on an issue from a story that will form the basis of a debate.

2. First, list all the episodes in the story that could be debated. For instance, the way a character handles a conflict or a decision made by a character that affects the lives of the other characters.

3. Now choose one of the episodes and write three statements for and three statements against the way it was handled.

4. When writing an argument 'for', you will need to write the reasons why you agree with the way the situation was handled. When writing arguments 'against' you will need to write the reasons why you disagree with the way the situation was handled. Make sure your arguments for both sides are clear and logical.

5. Proofread your work carefully and present your debate to your teacher. Find other children who have also read the book and see whether they agree with your arguments.

# Everybody Wants to Be a Critic

1. After reading a book, prepare a review of the story stating whether, in your opinion, the book should or should not be read.

2. Think about why you did or did not enjoy reading the story. Write a list of the things that helped you formulate your opinion. For instance, was there a strong plot? Were the characters well developed? Was the story exciting or boring? Why do you think so?

3. Now, using your list, write an argument convincing people to read or not to read the story. Your argument should be clearly written and show examples from the text.

4. When you have completed your first draft, book a conference with your teacher. Your teacher will show you ways of improving your argument.

5. Finally, present your argument to your classmates. Did your argument convince your classmates to read or not read the story?

# Character of the Week

1. Collect a few books that you have read and make a list of all the characters you have encountered who deserve an award for good behaviour.

2. Now, write each character's name with a brief description of their good deed.

3. Design an award certificate either on a computer using a graphics program or by hand using coloured pencils, felt-tipped pens, paints or pastels. Make sure you write why the character is receiving this award.

4. Draw or scan a picture of the character and organise a display of these portraits. Pin the award certificate beside each character.

# Book Cards

1. Put together a collection of books you have read. You will use information about these books to make a display of posters for your local library or school library.

2. First, write a description of each title. This should include information about the setting, the plot, the characters, the theme and why you liked that particular title. Search the Internet for photos of the authors and biographical information about them, including other books they have written.

3. Proofread your work carefully and use a graphics program such as *Publisher*, *Kid Pix* or *Hyperstudio* to publish your final copy. Print the information and if possible have the posters laminated.

4. Set up a display in the school library or obtain permission from your community library to display your posters alongside the books you have written about.

# What Would it Be Like?

1. In this activity you are going to think about what it would be like to be a part of the story you have read.

2. First, create a table in *Word* with two columns and two rows so that you have a square with four boxes. In the first box, write the heading 'Character'. Choose a character from the story and write what it would be like to be that character.

3. In the second box, write the heading 'Neighbourhood'. Now write what it would be like to live in the neighbourhood described in the story.

4. In the third box, write the heading 'Author'. Write what it would be like to be the author of the story. Include information such as why you think the author wrote this story.

5. In the last box, write the heading 'Conflict'. Write how you would have dealt with the conflict in the story.

6. Proofread your work carefully then discuss it with your teacher.

# What's the Point?

1. Most stories have a theme. This is where an author explores an issue through the characters and the plot.

2. Choose a story that you have read and determine the theme. Begin writing a report. Answering these questions may help shape your report.
   - What was the author trying to say through the story?
   - How successful was the author in getting the message across to you, the reader?
   - In what ways do you think that reading this story has enabled you to understand others?

3. Read your final published report to your classmates along with a brief oral synopsis of the story. Finish off by either recommending or not recommending the book to your classmates.

# Picture This!

1. When you have finished reading a story, decide on a part of the story you would like to paint.

   It could be:
   - your favourite episode
   - an exciting section
   - the setting
   - the theme of the story
   - the conflict between the characters
   - the solution to the story's conflict.

2. When you have decided, plan the details of your painting. Will your painting be realistic or abstract? Sketch the details lightly with greylead pencil before you begin painting.

3. When you have completed your masterpiece, present it to your classmates. Explain why you chose to paint that particular section of the story and how it fits into the overall plot.

# Ratings

1. In this activity you will be giving aspects of a story a 'thumbs up' or a 'thumbs down' and giving reasons for your choice.

2. Below is a list of things to do with the story. Rate each one by giving it thumbs up for a positive response or a thumbs down for a negative response. You must also justify your responses by giving the reasons behind your thoughts.

   • the main character
   • the minor characters
   • the plot
   • the setting
   • the illustrations
   • the beginning
   • the ending

3. The way you present the final copy is entirely up to you, but make sure you proofread your work carefully. Display your final copy alongside a copy of the book for others to read.

# Assessment and Record Keeping

The purpose of assessment is to gather and then analyse information about students' performance in a variety of contexts. Ongoing evaluation provides important feedback to students, staff, parents and others who have a vested interest in the development of the child. The primary aim of assessing the tasks presented in this book is to evaluate students' understanding of story structure through the use of higher-order thinking skills. This can be achieved in a number of ways, including checklists, reading journals, conferences, sharing and presenting, and work samples.

# Methods of Assessment

The purpose of assessment is to gather and then analyse information about students' performance in a variety of contexts. Ongoing evaluation provides important feedback to students, staff, parents and others who have a vested interest in the development of the child.

Record keeping is also a cyclic process involving teachers and students in observing and recording growth and learning progress over time. The teacher and the student share the responsibility for maintaining the records.

The primary aim of assessing the tasks presented in this book is to evaluate students' understanding of story structure through the use of higher-order thinking skills. This can be achieved in a number of ways, including checklists, reading journals, conferences, sharing and presenting, and work samples.

## *Checklists*

Checklists provide a means of recording students' work. They allow teachers to track activities students have completed, as well as monitoring and documenting student growth and understanding over time. Although checklists lack detailed information, they do provide a basic insight into student achievement at a glance.

## *Reading Journals*

Reading journals enable children to record and document their personal responses to the texts they read. (See figure 5). They may contain lists of and responses to books students have read, activities they have completed, details of individual or group conferences, skills checklists and some form of self-assessment where students reflect upon their own learning and achievements.

## *Conferences*

A scheduled conference enables a teacher to work one on one or with a group of students exploring and discussing a number of issues relating to story structure, the use of reading strategies and the thinking behind students' responses to texts. A conference is also a great opportunity to check and evaluate the student's reading journal, to keep students on task and to assist students in selecting reading tasks appropriate to the text and to their ability.

Students do most of the talking in a conference. The teacher's role is to listen, respond, question and take anecdotal notes for assessment purposes. A reading conference folder containing student and teacher notes is essential because it provides a record of the student's reading progress.

During a conference, notes can be made on:

• the types of strategies the student is using in oral reading

• the student's level of comprehension and how they analyse the story

• the student's personal responses to the text

• the literacy needs of the student

• how the student responds to open-ended questions.

Bloom's taxonomy can be of great use in a conference. Questions formulated according to the different levels of thinking can be incorporated in every conference (see pages 88 and 89).

 #HB-9653 © 2003 Hawker Brownlow Education

# *Analysis of Story Structure*

The following tables offer some questions that can be used in a conference. They are useful in evaluating and determining a student's understanding of story structure.

| Plot Analysis | Character Analysis | Setting Analysis |
|---|---|---|
| What were the main events in the story? | Who are the main characters? How do you know? | Where does the story take place? |
| What was the most exciting part in the story? Why do you think so? | Are the minor characters important to the story? Why or why not? | When does the story take place? |
| Did the story have a good ending? | Is the character experiencing some kind of conflict? What is it and how is it resolved? | How important is the setting to the story? |
| How would you have altered the ending? | | How does the setting in the story differ from the world we live in? |
| Did you like the beginning of the story? Why or why not? | Are the characters likeable? | Is the story set in a real place or a place of fantasy? |
| | Were there any characters you disliked? Why? | |
| Describe the way the plot develops throughout the story. How do the events at the beginning of the book lead to the ending? | Describe the relationship between the characters. | Find and read aloud a passage in the book that truly describes the setting. |
| | Compare and contrast two of the characters. | Prepare a list of words the author uses to describe the setting. |
| Were you able to predict the ending? Why or why not? | What is this character's role in the story? | |
| What would you change to make the story better? | Does this character change at all during the story? In what way? | How would the setting be different if it was set in the future? Would it change the story in any important way? |
| Make a list of the events as they occurred in the story. | | Does the setting alter in any way during the story? How does this impact on the story-line? |
| What events could not have happened if the text was based on fact? | How would you change the characters' personalities? | |
| | List the positive and negative attributes of the main character. | Does the setting affect the characters in any way? |
| Compare and contrast the plot of two books in the same genre. | | |

| Style Analysis | Theme Analysis | Mood Analysis |
|---|---|---|
| Discuss a particular scene that sticks in your mind.<br><br>Have you been left with a mental picture of the story? Describe this picture to the group.<br><br>In your opinion, how well has the story been written? Be prepared to elaborate in your discussion.<br><br>Discuss a particular descriptive passage the author has written that describes either a character or a setting.<br><br>What interesting words did the author use when describing the characters?<br><br>What was it about the story that made you want to read until the end?<br><br>Does the author like the characters they have created? How can you tell?<br><br>Compare and contrast the style of two books written by the same author.<br><br>Explain how you would have solved the main character's problem.<br><br>Compare the main character's personality at the start with that at the end of the story. | What was the author trying to say to us in this story?<br><br>Is there a moral or lesson to be learnt in the story? What is it?<br><br>What is the relationship between the plot and the theme of the story?<br><br>Why do you think the author wrote this story? What point were they trying to make?<br><br>Could this story happen in real life? Why or why not?<br><br>How is this story different to real-life experiences?<br><br>Does the author clearly state their point of view in the story? | How did you feel while reading the story? For example, did you feel happy, excited, sad?<br><br>What happened in the story to make you feel a certain way?<br><br>What do you remember most about the story? Why?<br><br>Does the mood of the story change in any way?<br><br>How do you think the author felt about their characters?<br><br>Does the author favour one character over another? How can you tell?<br><br>How do the illustrations help reflect the mood of the story?<br><br>Write a list of words that describe the mood of the story. Present this list to the group.<br><br>What emotions did the characters display throughout the story? Make a list of these. |

 #HB-9653 © 2003 Hawker Brownlow Education

# Sharing and Presenting

The presentation of final and published tasks is an essential element of a literature program. In addition to allowing the presenter to become a role model for other students, it also provides another avenue for assessing and recording student achievement. As the student presents the task to the class, the teacher can observe, question and take notes on a variety of aspects, including:

• the student's understanding of the text

• the appropriateness of the task

• the student's interaction with the audience

• the student's level of confidence. (Does the student regularly attempt the same type of task or is the student prepared to take risks and attempt something more challenging?)

• the student's knowledge of story structure (plot, characterisation, setting, theme, mood, style, illustrations, genre and so on)

• the student's preferred thinking level

• how well the student writes, spells and understands the mechanics of writing.

Sharing and presenting work can be of immense value to the audience. Many skills and strategies can be learnt incidentally through audience participation. Some of these come from:

• being introduced to a variety of texts

• viewing completed tasks

• getting new ideas

• having the opportunity to question, listen and observe

• being a part of a cooperative learning community

• developing the ability to constructively judge and evaluate other students' work.

# Work Samples

Students' work samples that can be included in an English portfolio are an excellent way of showcasing students' progress and achievement over the year. A portfolio will contain evidence of the student's performance in, and understanding of, a variety of learning experiences and tasks. It will highlight strengths, include comments from the student and the teacher and become a valuable reporting tool to share with parents.

The portfolio might contain a completed task from each of the six thinking levels or focus on the elements of story structure or a combination of both. By involving students in the selection and evaluation of work samples the experience becomes much more meaningful and valuable.

# *Reading Inventory*

Name _____

**What kind of books do you like to read?**

_____

_____

_____

_____

**Who are your favourite authors?**

_____

**Who are your favourite illustrators?**

_____

**Which are your favourite books?**

_____

**List two books you have read recently.**

_____

_____

**Do you like to read? (Why? Why not?)**

_____

_____

_____

_____

_____

**Do you have any books of your own at home?**

_____

_____

**Do you ever borrow books from the local library?**

_____

_____

# *Reading Journal*

**Name** _____

**Book Details**

**Title** _____

**Author** _____

**Illustrator (where applicable):** _____

**Genre** _____

**I started reading this book on** _____

**I finished reading this book on** _____

**My Thoughts on this Book:**

_____

_____

_____

_____

_____

_____

_____

_____

_____

_____

_____

_____

_____

_____

_____

_____

**Work Requirements (Fill this in during the conference with your teacher.)**

**The activity I choose to do on this book is:**

_____

_____

**Student Self-Evaluation (Fill this out after you have done the activity.)**

**What I think I learnt doing this activity:**

_____

_____

_____

_____

**What I think I would do differently if I did this activity again:**

_____

_____

_____

_____

**Improvements I need to make in my reading:**

_____

_____

_____

_____

**Teacher Comments**

_____

_____

_____

_____

_____

_____

_____

_____

_____

# Checklists

## *Knowledge Tasks*

| Name of Student | Readers' Theatre | Felt Board | Postcard | Slide Show | Story Map | Storyteller | Word Puzzles | Bookmark | Story Poster | Character Mobiles |
|---|---|---|---|---|---|---|---|---|---|---|
| | | | | | | | | | | |
| | | | | | | | | | | |
| | | | | | | | | | | |
| | | | | | | | | | | |
| | | | | | | | | | | |
| | | | | | | | | | | |
| | | | | | | | | | | |
| | | | | | | | | | | |
| | | | | | | | | | | |
| | | | | | | | | | | |
| | | | | | | | | | | |
| | | | | | | | | | | |
| | | | | | | | | | | |
| | | | | | | | | | | |
| | | | | | | | | | | |
| | | | | | | | | | | |
| | | | | | | | | | | |
| | | | | | | | | | | |
| | | | | | | | | | | |
| | | | | | | | | | | |
| | | | | | | | | | | |
| | | | | | | | | | | |
| | | | | | | | | | | |
| | | | | | | | | | | |
| | | | | | | | | | | |
| | | | | | | | | | | |
| | | | | | | | | | | |

# Comprehension Tasks

| Name of Student | Who's Who | Talkfest | Lift the Flap | Keeping Track | Game Time | Fave Ravve | Design a Set | Comic Capers | Character Traits | Acting Up! |
|---|---|---|---|---|---|---|---|---|---|---|
| | | | | | | | | | | |
| | | | | | | | | | | |
| | | | | | | | | | | |
| | | | | | | | | | | |
| | | | | | | | | | | |
| | | | | | | | | | | |
| | | | | | | | | | | |
| | | | | | | | | | | |
| | | | | | | | | | | |
| | | | | | | | | | | |
| | | | | | | | | | | |
| | | | | | | | | | | |
| | | | | | | | | | | |
| | | | | | | | | | | |
| | | | | | | | | | | |
| | | | | | | | | | | |
| | | | | | | | | | | |
| | | | | | | | | | | |
| | | | | | | | | | | |
| | | | | | | | | | | |
| | | | | | | | | | | |
| | | | | | | | | | | |
| | | | | | | | | | | |
| | | | | | | | | | | |
| | | | | | | | | | | |
| | | | | | | | | | | |

## Application Tasks

| Name of Student | Holidays! | Let's Celebrate | On the Scene Reporter | Playing Games | Puppet Show | Windows into Worlds | A Model Character | Cover Up! | Story Starters | Word Collage |
|---|---|---|---|---|---|---|---|---|---|---|
| | | | | | | | | | | |
| | | | | | | | | | | |
| | | | | | | | | | | |
| | | | | | | | | | | |
| | | | | | | | | | | |
| | | | | | | | | | | |
| | | | | | | | | | | |
| | | | | | | | | | | |
| | | | | | | | | | | |
| | | | | | | | | | | |
| | | | | | | | | | | |
| | | | | | | | | | | |
| | | | | | | | | | | |
| | | | | | | | | | | |
| | | | | | | | | | | |
| | | | | | | | | | | |
| | | | | | | | | | | |
| | | | | | | | | | | |
| | | | | | | | | | | |
| | | | | | | | | | | |
| | | | | | | | | | | |
| | | | | | | | | | | |
| | | | | | | | | | | |
| | | | | | | | | | | |
| | | | | | | | | | | |
| | | | | | | | | | | |
| | | | | | | | | | | |

# Analysis Tasks

| Name of Student | What Are they Really Like? | Wanted! | Under the Microscope | Step Right Up! | Maybe … Maybe Not … | What Would Happen If … | Dear Author | Back to the Past | An Interview with … | This Is your Life … |
|---|---|---|---|---|---|---|---|---|---|---|
| | | | | | | | | | | |
| | | | | | | | | | | |
| | | | | | | | | | | |
| | | | | | | | | | | |
| | | | | | | | | | | |
| | | | | | | | | | | |
| | | | | | | | | | | |
| | | | | | | | | | | |
| | | | | | | | | | | |
| | | | | | | | | | | |
| | | | | | | | | | | |
| | | | | | | | | | | |
| | | | | | | | | | | |
| | | | | | | | | | | |
| | | | | | | | | | | |
| | | | | | | | | | | |
| | | | | | | | | | | |
| | | | | | | | | | | |
| | | | | | | | | | | |
| | | | | | | | | | | |
| | | | | | | | | | | |
| | | | | | | | | | | |
| | | | | | | | | | | |
| | | | | | | | | | | |
| | | | | | | | | | | |
| | | | | | | | | | | |
| | | | | | | | | | | |

## *Synthesis Tasks*

| Name of Student | A New Cover | If Only … | Introducing … | A Poem | Story Props and Models | Dear Diary | A Song | Who's Next Door? | A Picture Says a Thousand Words | Presenting … |
|---|---|---|---|---|---|---|---|---|---|---|
| | | | | | | | | | | |
| | | | | | | | | | | |
| | | | | | | | | | | |
| | | | | | | | | | | |
| | | | | | | | | | | |
| | | | | | | | | | | |
| | | | | | | | | | | |
| | | | | | | | | | | |
| | | | | | | | | | | |
| | | | | | | | | | | |
| | | | | | | | | | | |
| | | | | | | | | | | |
| | | | | | | | | | | |
| | | | | | | | | | | |
| | | | | | | | | | | |
| | | | | | | | | | | |
| | | | | | | | | | | |
| | | | | | | | | | | |
| | | | | | | | | | | |
| | | | | | | | | | | |
| | | | | | | | | | | |
| | | | | | | | | | | |
| | | | | | | | | | | |
| | | | | | | | | | | |
| | | | | | | | | | | |

## *Evaluation Tasks*

| Name of Student | You Win Some You Lose Some | You Be the Judge | For and Against | Everybody Wants to Be a Critic | Character of the Week | Book Cards | What Would it Be Like? | What's the Point? | Picture This! | Ratings |
|---|---|---|---|---|---|---|---|---|---|---|
| | | | | | | | | | | |
| | | | | | | | | | | |
| | | | | | | | | | | |
| | | | | | | | | | | |
| | | | | | | | | | | |
| | | | | | | | | | | |
| | | | | | | | | | | |
| | | | | | | | | | | |
| | | | | | | | | | | |
| | | | | | | | | | | |
| | | | | | | | | | | |
| | | | | | | | | | | |
| | | | | | | | | | | |
| | | | | | | | | | | |
| | | | | | | | | | | |
| | | | | | | | | | | |
| | | | | | | | | | | |
| | | | | | | | | | | |
| | | | | | | | | | | |
| | | | | | | | | | | |
| | | | | | | | | | | |
| | | | | | | | | | | |
| | | | | | | | | | | |
| | | | | | | | | | | |
| | | | | | | | | | | |
| | | | | | | | | | | |
| | | | | | | | | | | |

#HB-9653 © 2003 Hawker Brownlow Education